To Denise

A seasonal cottage is a state of mind. Live the life you love.

Barbara

Waterside Cottages

Waterside Cottages

Barbara Jacksier
Photography by Dan Mayers

GIBBS SMITH
TO ENRICH AND INSPIRE HUMANKIND

Salt Lake City | Charleston | Santa Fe | Santa Barbara

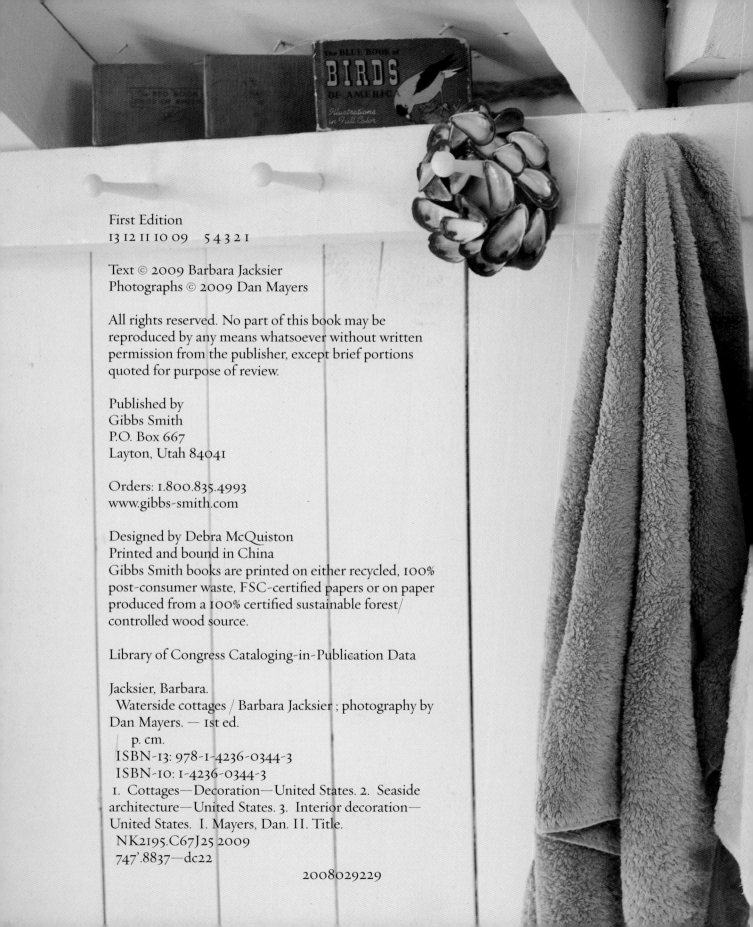

First Edition
13 12 11 10 09   5 4 3 2 1

Published by
Gibbs Smith
P.O. Box 667
Layton, Utah 84041

Orders: 1.800.835.4993
www.gibbs-smith.com

Designed by Debra McQuiston
Printed and bound in China
Gibbs Smith books are printed on either recycled, 100%
post-consumer waste, FSC-certified papers or on paper
produced from a 100% certified sustainable forest/
controlled wood source.

Library of Congress Cataloging-in-Publication Data

Jacksier, Barbara.
  Waterside cottages / Barbara Jacksier ; photography by
Dan Mayers. — 1st ed.
    p. cm.
  ISBN-13: 978-1-4236-0344-3
  ISBN-10: 1-4236-0344-3
  1. Cottages—Decoration—United States. 2. Seaside
architecture—United States. 3. Interior decoration—
United States. I. Mayers, Dan. II. Title.
  NK2195.C67J25 2009
  747'.8837—dc22
                              2008029229

contents

Acknowledgments

It takes a lot of help to take an idea and turn it into a printed book. *Waterside Cottages* would not have been possible without the eagle eyes of the "scouts" who helped us find the gorgeous waterside homes featured here; the kindness of the homeowners who opened their houses and hearts to us; the dedication of our editor, Lisa Anderson, the designer, Debra McQuiston, and the production department and marketing staff at Gibbs Smith; and the unfailing support of our families. We'd also like to thank the McCauley family for letting us photograph in their Marin County, California cottage (pages 2 and 7).

For leading us to many of the cottages we profiled, we are grateful to Anna Ball, Rich Blumm, Christine Mumma Booth, Jackie Carnegie, Sara Evans, Aubré Duncan, Joan Gordon, Sunday Hendrickson, Suzie and Mark Holt, Lisa Miller, Nancy King Monk, Fifi O'Neill, Alison Wells, and Jeff West.

The seeds of inspiration for this book were sown during the time we traveled coast to coast, photographing homes for *Cottage Style* magazine. Thank you, Stan Harris, Phyllis Goldstein, Diane Speros, and Ellen Wolynec, for your support during that time.

Dan extends a huge thank-you to all the homeowners who allowed him to enter their lives and explore their creativity as he photographed their homes. He thanks Misha and Lola for their support with all of his travels and life. He also thanks his parents for encouraging his love of the ocean.

For setting up her Web site (www.barbarajacksier.com) and The Book Blog (www.barbarajacksier.blogspot.com), Barbara thanks Fred Jacksier-Chasen and fellow blogger Tara Frey. For her continual inspiration, Barbara is grateful to Renita Steinberg and the Ruetenik-Hudson family. She is truly indebted to Ruth Jacksier and her dog, Belgium, for being her most ardent supporters through thick and thin. Finally, she thanks Everett Chasen for his continual help, encouragement, and editorial support. Let's do it again soon!

Preface

Looking through photos of homes that we considered for inclusion in this book, photographer Dan Mayers and I asked ourselves the same questions over and over again. Would arriving at the cottage make us feel like trading in our ordinary shoes for flip flops? Did the kitchen and dining areas give us a hint that fresh-caught lobster, shrimp fritters, or grilled catch-of-the-day might be on the menu? Were there any unique coastal cues in the way the living room and bedrooms were decorated?

In other words, was it possible to tell the home was located on the shore of a lake, river, or ocean—without seeing the view from the window?

The thirteen houses we selected differ greatly in their decorating schemes, but all have the ability to instantly transport you to the water's edge. Some are centuries old and others were built recently. A few boast vibrant Caribbean colors or nautical hues, while others rely on an all-white palette for a sense of serenity. Some feature rooms filled with coastal keepsakes and accumulated treasures; others celebrate simplicity.

Whether they are primary residences, artist's retreats, or weekend getaways, all of the cottages in this book offer their owners and guests a place to enjoy time together, to chill out, and to feel sheltered and protected from the raging sea and the world outside. We hope you'll share our discoveries of new and creative ways to translate a love of waterside surroundings into successful decorating schemes using creative design solutions.

Barbara Jacksier

Introduction

What is it that draws generation after generation to land's end? Nearly all who dwell by the shore will tell you the pleasures of hearing the rhythm of waves or watching the sunset over the water far outweigh any inconveniences.

Salt sticks in the shakers, humidity ruins porch furniture, garden roses wither from salt spray—still there's something irresistible about living by the water.

As if countering the vastness of mighty oceans, most of those who live on America's coastlines have historically built homes of small proportions on snug lots. Although architectural styles vary greatly, these petite waterside dwellings are generally referred to as cottages or bungalows. Their exteriors are frequently painted in sun-reflecting whites, nautical blues, or whimsical colors.

The interiors of these houses likewise avoid formality in favor of a casual approach. For many cottage owners, the goal is to create the illusion that their décor is somehow "thrown together," albeit very tastefully.

Even in homes designed by professionals, there's always a place for "found objects" in a seaside home. Small details—such as sea urchins casually piled in an antique bowl or a bookcase display of sand pails—are what truly give cottages that elusive quality known as coziness.

Since old-fashioned summer cottages were often furnished with sturdy but past-its-prime furniture, today's cottage owners seek to replicate that spirit through flea market finds. Whitewashed antique four-poster beds or seating cloaked in washable fish print slipcovers can give any room the kind of atmosphere that brings back bygone days of childhood shore vacations.

To add to the summery mood, bare wood floors are often punctuated with sisal mats or hand-painted floor cloths. Windows are left undressed—as long as shading from the sun is not required. When necessary, gauze panels or plantation shutters effectively filter the sun without blocking the view.

Cottages used as weekend getaways and vacation retreats spotlight design features encouraging residents and guests to relax and unwind. A croquet set on the lawn, boxes of old-fashioned board games stacked near a table, or a shelf of old books waiting for new readers all hold the promise of simple fun. These amusements offer a trip down memory lane for older generations—and a new kind of thrill for today's "plugged in" young people.

A serene blue and white color scheme unites this California cottage's interior with the water surrounding the property.

A giant clamshell makes a fitting container for an assortment of sparkling sea glass in shades of frosty white, blue, and green.

Getting Waterside Style

Waterside style need not be—and often is not—confined to residences within walking distance of an ocean or lake. Several attributes define successful coastal decorating, and anyone, anywhere, can create a casual waterfront atmosphere, even when the nearest body of water is a thousand miles away!

Choosing colors compatible with ocean views; adding patterns to your furniture and walls that evoke the water or waterfront activities; keeping your decorating scheme simple; using materials associated with the sea; finding antiques that have aged gracefully; prominently displaying items, like seashells and sea glass, found on beaches; and collecting maritime memorabilia are all elements the owners of the homes in this book have successfully mastered.

Here are some ideas common to these wonderful homes you can use to create your own dream waterfront home, wherever it may be.

Water colors are complex blends of numerous tones. Mix an array of seaside blues with aquatic greens for a tranquil effect.

Choose Coastal Colors

Color is intrinsic to waterside style. The color of a room is what you notice most upon entry . . . or least. When a room's colors are done right, you don't think about it—you feel it.

Take your cue from the rolling surf and decorate your walls in sea blues and greens; or evoke the Fourth of July and design a red, white, and blue haven. Mix and match sand shades for a neutral palette, or concoct a potent Caribbean-style cock-

tail by using mango gold, passion fruit pink, or Key West lime. Each palette offers a distinctive take on waterside style.

When choosing colors for your home, always consider the clarity of the hues. Think of colors you've noticed near the water on a sunny day. Look for crystal clear blues and greens, glowing tans, or tropical brights. Muted rainy day colors, such as ones dulled down with gray or brown, should be avoided, as they look more urban.

Embellished with whimsical flip-flops, this custom-made daybed exudes sassy beachcomber style.

Play with Patterns

Among the types of wallpaper, decals, and fabrics you can find to add seaside or lakeside are realistic renditions of shells and subtle coral patterns, those with wriggling trout, and fanciful flamingos. Hula girls, ships' flags, and historic lighthouse patterns can be found online, along with nearly anything else you can imagine.

Think small by using narrow border prints or individual paste-on wall appliqués at chair rail height; or think large by finding room for a wall-size mural of your favorite Hawaiian surfing locale or shore vista.

Repeat your chosen motif on upholstery fabrics, or introduce new themes through cushions that change with the seasons. For continuity, try creating a house-wide theme inspired by the South Pacific, denizens of the deep, or vintage sailing vessels.

If you're not ready to commit to a full-scale decorating theme, get your feet wet with inexpensive accents that evoke waterside activities. Toss colorful flip-flops into a basket by the back door. Hang framed photographs, paintings, or prints of dunes, docks, and fishing boats. Place stacks of books on nautical history, shore birds, or aquatic sports on side tables. Toss pillows stitched in regatta stripes on folding wooden deck chairs for seaworthy outdoor seating.

Outside, display a hand-painted sign welcoming your guests to the beach, or one that advertises fresh lobsters. After dark, light up your garden or illuminate a walkway to the shore with nautical lanterns or tiki torches.

An unexpected mix of pale wood and timeworn white items forms an important part of the eclectic cottage look.

A humble stair gets a decorative lift. Contrasting textures, instead of color, add drama to this vertical vignette.

Try Simplicity

Coastal colors and patterns are not the only way to anchor your cottage to the shore. Simplicity is a serene and charming option for a decorating motif and can be used in any room of the house.

Limit your color palette to ensure that nothing interferes with the real focus of your home—the people who live in or visit it and the beautiful scenery that surrounds it.

For a peaceful monochromatic color scheme, combine a variety of cream tones, tinted shades, and distressed whites. It's best to steer clear of stark modern whites, which can look cold and uninviting. Prefer a hint of color? Mix officer's whites with crisp nautical blues or soft greens.

Pare down furnishings to the essentials and be selective in choosing accessories. For a home that feels like a calm retreat, toss washable white or pale slipcovers over upholstered sofas and chairs. Gauzy drapes, roll-up shades, or simple tie back curtains lend an air of effortlessness to cottage windows. If you have wood floors, roll up the rugs.

Functional items that do double duty as decorative accents cut down on clutter. For example, everyday items imbued with coastal flair, such as ocean-themed dishes or aqua vases, can be displayed throughout the house until pressed into service. If there's an ocean, lake or other interesting feature nearby, call attention to it by placing a telescope at a window. Remember, in waterfront decorating, less is often more!

Rustic yet charming, old-fashioned wood plank walls create a visual contrast to nostalgic displays and vintage finds.

A painted floral headboard and table coverings dripping in beads have a vintage look set against a soothing blue background.

Borrow Seaworthy Textures

In some areas, waterside cottages were originally built using the same maritime materials and craftsmen employed at nearby shipyards. Interior walls were fashioned from sheets of marine plywood and then partially or entirely covered with shiplap beadboard, if money and time allowed.

Today, authentic tongue-and-groove beadboard (available from millwork specialists) and less expensive grooved paneling sheets (available at home centers) can replicate this look.

Other rough or three-dimensional textures traditionally associated with seaside cottages include smooth sailcloth window awnings and knotted sailor's hammocks. Introduce a tropical surface treatment by using bamboo or grasscloth wallpaper or woven sisal, reed, or straw floor mats.

Smooth surfaces that mimic water on a calm day are also appropriate. Glass that captures the depths of the sea adds a magical quality to a room. It looks different at different times of day and in different weather. When choosing glass for a backsplash, countertop, or edging, consider its color as well as its thickness. Density and composition determine the sense of movement you see when light reflects off the surface. Look for glass with embedded bubbles and wavy finishes for dazzling effects.

Materials for walkways and garden paths that play up the proximity to or the illusion of water include crushed clam or oyster shells and wooden plank boardwalks with rope railings.

This mix of genuine antiques and moderately priced secondhand finds strikes a perfect balance between casual and classic.

Serve up a taste of fond vacation memories. Use souvenir tablecloths at mealtime or as colorful curtains or cushions.

Create a Sense of Age

The coziest cottage interiors rely on vintage pieces. Old fashioned in the very best sense of the word, these furnishings and accessories are reminiscent of simpler times and less demanding lifestyles. It doesn't matter where nostalgic items come from. Your grandmother's attic or an eBay auction are both fine sources, but what matters is the feelings the pieces evoke.

Even if you are decorating a cottage you only visit on weekends or vacations, the rooms should feel lived in. Mixing and matching items found at local antique shops, flea markets, and tag sales invests your home's decor with one-of-a-kind personality. To establish an easy-going, laid-back lifestyle, nothing should be too fragile to be off-limits. Vintage plates, bowls, and cups are there to be used. Sentimental board games and books are not just accessories—they're an integral part of rainy day activities.

Even a newly built home can lie about its age when its surfaces appear weathered by time. Beadboard rescued from demolition sites or discarded gems that have been repurposed are ideal. Include at least one gently restored piece from the past, or place a sentimental cluster of classic items in every room. When something old isn't practical, shop for newly crafted pieces with a faux patina or distressed surface. Like a cherished scrapbook, possessions that appear to have been assembled over time are well suited to a home decorated in cottage style.

No matter where you call home, a shell garland strung on a bed, mantel, or mirror creates the illusion of a seaside dwelling.

The best displays, like the best cottages, are humble and unpretentious. Fill inexpensive bottles with sand, shells, and pebbles.

Display Found Objects

Everyone who spends time at the shore has a collection of special found objects. Reinforce your home's real or imagined connection to the water by displaying glass jars filled with shells or river rocks. Starfish make a terrific table accent: any room gains a seaside view when you line a window ledge with a parade of starfish or hang a garland of shells.

Mixing shells with sea glass is a great way to add extra sparkle to your arrangements. Tumbled by waves and wind, these irregularly-shaped chunks of glass come in a variety of sun-softened shades—cobalt blue from old glass jars and bottles; browns from patent medicines, sodas, and beers; and greens and turquoise from old glass insulators and canning jars.

For a nautically themed centerpiece, place easy-to-make rope and twine sailor's knots in a favorite bowl or basket.

Collect postcards associated with your favorite vacation spot or trawl for cards with marine life motifs or ocean views.

Display Collectibles

Collectibles associated with vacation pastimes or destinations are ideal for creating nostalgic vignettes. Stock a curio cabinet with carved duck decoys, America's Cup memorabilia, or tools of the maritime trades. Sprinkle a shadowbox coffee table with sand; then place miniature sailboats and sand toys on top. Recall bygone beach days with a collage of vintage postcards or through a pyramid of colorful oyster cans.

Collect inexpensive critters crafted entirely of tiny shells or exquisite mirrors framed with treasures from the sea. If you can't find the perfect accent, make your own artistic masterpieces. Shell-encrusted boxes, for example, are easy to make: spread a thick layer of glue or self-hardening clay on the box or other object to be embellished and simply push in the shells. When the glue dries, add more glue or clay around heavy shells to hold them in place. Most craft shops sell bags of seashells.

Just Relax

In today's fast-paced world, creating a home that helps you and your family slow down is more important than ever. Drawing inspiration from traditional coastal cottages is a terrific way to create a comfortable and comforting décor, whether decorating a weekend getaway or a year-round home.

Remember, coastal design isn't a style, it's an attitude. The homes in this book all have it, and with just a little bit of work, your home can have it too.

Boathouse
On the River

Hugging the shores of the Kalamazoo River and Lake Michigan, the tiny town of Saugatuck, Michigan, was originally founded in the 1800s as a *lumber camp*. In 1910, a small group of painters from the Art Institute of Chicago opened a summer painting school there called the Oxbow School. Attracted by the scenic dunes, *sandy beaches,* and pristine forests, a thriving artists' colony quickly developed in Saugatuck, featuring *romantic cottages,* picturesque boathouses and docks, and a welcoming *lakeshore community.*

A newly added dockside deck, *left*, sporting a fabric market umbrella from Pier 1 and cushions from Target, is the perfect spot to read the morning paper or enjoy a twilight drink. **An outdoor shower**, *below*, transcends time, which makes it all the more special. **The cottage's deck**, *facing*, serves as an extra seating and dining area and offers a panoramic view of the boathouse and river below.

"Cozy cottages are by far my favorite type

Today, one of the few remaining boathouses can be found perched on a steep bank of the Kalamazoo, just across from a nature preserve that now surrounds the still-flourishing art school. John Cannarsa and his partner, Jeff Phillips, noticed the building when they passed it by on their boat.

"The boathouse is a pretty unique structure for the area. That's because setback rules don't allow dwellings so close to the river anymore," John recalls.

The cottage it belonged to was hidden in the trees with a For Sale sign barely visible. They went back and looked at it from land but didn't even bother going inside—it was that bad. When it was still on the market a year later, Cannarsa and Phillips decided to check it out. After years of using their boat as a weekend home, they resolved to buy the property.

Both the main house and the boathouse were in pretty bad shape, but the boathouse was "screaming for attention," according to John. Years of erosion along the river's

steep forty-five degree bank had caused the structure to slip. John's design and construction management company, Cannarsa Structure and Design, shored up the boathouse's deteriorating foundation by jacking up the entire building, pouring new cement pilings, and setting the historic structure back down. Once they were sure the two-level boathouse would remain in the same location for many years to come, they had the structure's original Dutch lap siding repaired and painted espresso brown. A dilapidated roof was replaced with one of standing seam copper that will mirror the waterside setting once the metal ages and develops a blue-green patina.

"Cozy cottages are by far my favorite type of home—the more authentic, the better," says John. To that end, he peeled away layers of previous owners' "improvements and updates" from the upstairs main room, kitchenette, and bath. Out went a green shag carpet, revealing original pine floors.

of home — the more authentic, the better."

Ugly 1970s-era paneling, found both on the ceiling and the walls, was also removed, and beadboard was installed in its place. "Beadboard can be purchased at most lumber and home improvement centers, but it's important to get the type that has the larger grooves if you want a period look," John advises.

The walls were painted in soft yellow and minty green to recreate the mood of a casual 1920s retreat. "Though I usually use Benjamin Moore's ceramic flat paint, I used a semi-gloss on the walls to achieve a more cottage-like effect." Solid fabrics in blue, yellow, green, and red and cabana stripes in the same colors can be found on the bench cushions and pillows.

"We exposed the rafters and painted them in a light creamy color and painstakingly restored the old casement windows. There's simply nothing like wavy glass and true paned old windows," John explains. Keeping the wood cas-

ings bare contributes to the unpretentious nature of the main room.

Nautical memorabilia, including an antique first aid kit, a model sailboat, a life ring, and glass fishing floats evoke an old-time captain's quarters.

A rack of games, puzzles, Slinkys, and vintage books stand ready for a rainy afternoon, reminders of simpler times and childhood places. "A cottage bookshelf is a much better place to house my collection of Hardy Boys books than a storage box," John declares.

The kitchenette was retrofitted with a found drainboard sink and an old mini-stove. Instead of the usual under-sink cabinetry, a shirred curtain enhances the space's timeless quality. When John couldn't locate the sort of cabinets he wanted, he commissioned a local woodworker to recraft timeworn wood into rustic-style cabinets and then finish them with a brown glaze over a sand color. As a finishing

Living on a boat taught John to make the most of limited space. In the main room, he designed a window seat that opens to reveal a foldaway bed. The coffee table, an antique trunk, stores a set of bedding and is on casters.

touch, a classic light fixture with a pull chain hangs on the wall above the sink.

The lower level of the boathouse, which is smaller than the upper level, had been used solely as storage for boating gear for years. John and Jeff turned it into a snug getaway by adding a new bathroom, a changing room that leads to an outdoor shower, and a deck. "The deck provides space for a table and chairs, lounge chairs, and a copper firepit—and it gets us closer to the water," John says.

Because they had previously lived on a boat, John and Jeff knew how to make the most of every inch of space in the small structure. Several of their space-saving tricks are ingenious.

"I came up with the idea of buying just the internal workings of a sofa bed and having it built into a window seat," John proudly explains. "All you do is take off the seat cushion and pull up, just like a sofa bed."

John's favorite feature, however, is the boathouse's new outdoor shower. A screen fashioned from plantation shutters provides privacy from passing boat owners. "Showering outdoors is very liberating, especially in the early mornings when I feel as if I'm the only person around," John says.

Since the main cottage, their principal year-round residence, is not very large, the four-hundred-square-foot boathouse allows John, Jeff, and their dog, Cooper, to stretch their living space during all but the coldest months. It's a getaway destination for morning coffee, river watching, and naps—and a place to welcome guests in vintage style.

"This space reflects me," John concludes. "I like simplicity, and what we've created is a structure that's really simple, yet beautiful. I'm satisfied every time someone sees our boathouse and smiles, because I know they are seeing what I see."

Old-fashioned beadboard, *left*, painted a pale green, provides a casual background for an enamel drainboard sink, vintage mini stove, and nostalgic, but new, wall sconce from Lowe's home center. An inexpensive flat tension rod holds the under-sink curtain in place.

The lower level storage area, *below*, was transformed into shipshape sleeping quarters. John installed a checkerboard floor using Armstrong tiles. The vinyl squares are brand new, but the combination of black and terra-cotta produces a vintage look.

By the
Beautiful Sea

Alaska's snowy landscapes and ethereal northern lights are worlds apart
from the *sun and surf* of the Delaware shore. Yet Donna and

Glen Wade were living in Fairbanks when they first decided to build a
cottage in *Delaware's Bethany Beach.* A small seaside

town that has tried to keep out the high-rise condos and snarled traffic that
plague many of its neighbors, Bethany Beach is a quiet *family summer*
destination. The old-fashioned boardwalk looks

nearly the same as it did fifty years ago, when Donna's family spent many summers there.

Distressed white furnishings lend a newly

In 1970, Donna's parents retired to Bethany Beach. When one of her sisters built a cottage close by in 1995, Donna and Glen thought it made sense to build there as well.

"We thought of the house as investment property and intended to rent it out during the summer months. We only planned to use it for occasional long weekends and for an annual two-week family get-together," recalls Donna.

In 1998, the Wades purchased a lot from a well-respected local builder. It was a mere eight hundred yards from the Atlantic Ocean with a view of Indian River Bay. Donna wanted the exterior of the cottage they would build to have columns and a porch over a porch facade, a style popular in Charleston, South Carolina. On the upper level, a screened deck extends across the front of the house, encompassing an outdoor eating area and spacious sun porch.

For their interior floor plans, Donna and Glen used

a computer design CD. "Our goal was to have as many bedrooms as possible, to appeal to summer renters. I also wanted to have a large great room with a lot of space for entertaining and decks that faced the house's peaceful bay side," Donna adds.

During the six months that the cottage was under construction, the couple often communicated from Alaska with their builder by fax. "Talking on the phone was not always feasible due to the four-hour time difference," Donna explains. She made five cross-country trips to check on the building's progress.

On her first visit, Donna discovered an old medicine cabinet with peeling paint at an antique store. It was love at first sight. "That's when I decided how the house would be decorated. My mom, my aunt, and my sister Carole helped me hunt for good used furniture and accessories

built house an instant illusion of age.

with the same casual vintage style," she notes.

Donna and her family painted and distressed some of the pieces in country white and gave them a finish coat of Briwax. She wanted furniture and accessories that would lend the newly built house an instant illusion of age. Even new items like TV cabinets were painted to look old—and the knobs changed to those of vintage style.

While Donna chose a sun-bleached, whitewashed look throughout her house, she says she is not as dedicated to an all-white palette as sister Carole. Splashes of red, blue, and even silver define Donna's décor.

Each room in her house was assigned a subtle theme, which helped in the choice of accessories. For the nautical-style family room, the women bought vintage binoculars, lanterns, and sailboats. For the bedroom, decorated in a patriotic theme, they purchased a framed American flag

and other Fourth of July accents. "I rented a mini storage unit to hold everything that we bought until the house was ready," Donna says.

When the house was finished, Glen was delighted by how well the pieces, old and new, fit together. "My eye for size and placement of furniture and Carole's skill with detail and accessories make for a unique blend," Donna notes. "It does help to have a husband who can build a corner cabinet or sofa table the size you need—and a brother-in-law who can rewire old lamps and chandeliers!" she adds lovingly.

Donna and Glen loved everything about their new house—its proximity to family, its waterside location, and its lived-in, comfortable feeling. They loved it so much, Donna concedes, "We decided to retire and move in full time. So much for having an investment property!"

An open living space,
left, blends the cottage's living room, kitchen, and dining room. Donna hung architectural pieces to help define each area. Glen built the corner curio cabinet and sofa table and then rubbed the edges with sandpaper to age his newly crafted creations. **A small island,** *right*, faced with beadboard from Donna's grandmother's farmhouse is the focal point of the L-shaped kitchen. Glen planed down the wood, retaining a hint of historic paint. Old-fashioned pewter knobs and pulls grace the simple off-white cabinets, and vintage cooking utensils are on display. Concrete countertops add a rustic touch that balances the architectural pieces in the great room.

A white palette with natural

textures is fresh and warm.

For the family room, *right*, Donna chose a nautical motif with soft blue as her accent color. The handcrafted boat and several ships' lanterns are from the Shop of the Four Sisters (a home boutique Donna co-owns with her sisters). Donna painted the sailing vessel on the high seas and applied a crackle finish to make it look like an heirloom. Since the couple's four grandsons, nieces, and nephews visit often, washable cotton slipcovers top the Robin Bruce sofa and Ikea barrel chairs. **A large sixty-inch** round table, *facing*, dominates the indoor dining area. Sailcloth chair jackets are held in place with cabled cord loosely woven in and out of sail grommets. The patina of the metallic eyelets is echoed by a flea market chandelier repainted in burnished silver and pewter serving pieces.

For an authentic feel, retain hints of

historic paint when refinishing vintage pieces.

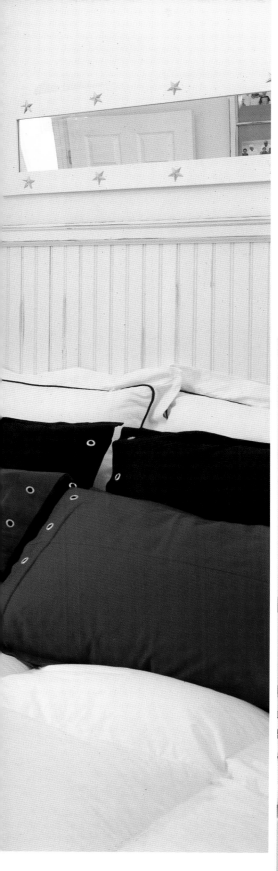

Flea market finds, *facing*, painted pristine white are given new life in the master bedroom. Glen built the headboard using beadboard and newel post millwork. In keeping with the room's patriotic theme, stars were glued onto the bureau knobs and the mirror frame.

With her young grandsons in mind, Donna outfitted one of the guestrooms, *above*, with twin berths. She used handsome striped fabrics to cover the padded plywood headboards, tailored dust ruffles, and shams. Adding striped piping to the contrasting pillows is the sort of little detail Donna's sister Carole insists on. While all of the bedrooms, *facing*, are primarily white, each has a different color scheme. In this guestroom, shades of gray and black add up to sophisticated sleeping quarters. Gauze drapes hung side by side in shades of silver and ivory frame the view. The wall-mounted bedside tables are painted wooden semi-circles atop fanciful wood brackets. Crowned with a fragment of architectural salvage, an old window frame flaunts a hand-painted sign above the bed.

BY THE BEAUTIFUL SEA

With doors that open to a
spectacular view on one
side and a comfy porch on
the other, the dining room is
simply furnished with a table
crafted of reclaimed wood
by a local woodworker. The
chairs are junk store acquisi-
tions made festive with paint
that coordinates with the
peppers in Missy's painting
above the mirror hutch.

An Island Refuge

Glossy red lobsters, hard shell steamer clams, delightful harbor scenes, and *weathered dinghies* are the subjects Maine artist Missy Asen loves to paint. Known for rendering *coastal themes* so realistically you can almost smell the brine, Missy's work is firmly anchored in New England's *maritime heritage.* The granddaughter of a sardine cannery owner, Missy's fondest childhood memories are of summers spent at her *grandparents' cottage* on Peaks Island in Casco Bay.

Sun-drenched colors add warmth to

While Peaks Island is one of the most densely settled of Portland's offshore vacation destinations, the house Missy shares with her husband, Michael, is on nearby Little Diamond Island, one of the least populated.

After spending several summers in a cottage so tiny that when Michael's three boys and their friends spent the night it felt like it might tip over, the couple decided to find a spot to build a bigger cottage. They didn't have far to look, since the island is just under a mile wide.

The land they found was on a secluded cove. It had once been the playground of a summer camp for orphans run by the Sisters of Mercy. The camp had been closed for many years when the Sisters decided to sell the vacant lot.

Collaborating with Portland architect Lee Hulst, the couple drew up plans for an eight-room cottage. The original design included a third-floor tower with a lookout. "When Lee told us that building the tower would put us over budget, I studied the blueprint for a minute and then placed my coffee mug on it. Using the curve of the mug as a guide, I drew an arch where the tower met the roof. That's why the roofline has an eyebrow arch. It's the type of quirky detail that the island's older houses have, and it kept us within our budget," Missy recalls.

Like many island dwellings, the Asens' cottage has hardwood floors, traditional beadboard walls, and a sense of family history. A double slate sink like the one in Missy's grandmother's house and a painted wooden sign from the restaurant her brother once owned add authenticity to the kitchen. "The owners of every salvage

a room even on the coldest days.

shop within a half-day's drive of Portland know Missy by name," Michael claims.

"I developed the ability to recognize a diamond in the rough, however," Missy counters. "For example, the corbels that accent the doorway in the front foyer came from a mainland house that was being demolished. They were covered in paint and pigeon feathers. When I told Michael I wanted to use them in the cottage, he thought I'd lost my mind. After I removed all of the gunk with a heat gun and chisel, even he admitted they were great."

The first floor's bold color scheme—sun drenched yellow, flamingo pink, and tidal pool turquoise—was another decision that Michael questioned at first. Missy chose paint by matching the colors to a swatch of upholstery fabric in a bright underwater print.

For the upstairs bedrooms, she employed the same palette but in more subdued shades. "I wanted a less intense, more restful look," she says.

Always happiest when surrounded by the sea, Missy brings the beach indoors by displaying bowls of sea glass, hanging fish-shaped lanterns, and adding new finds to a shadowbox table filled with urchins, starfish, and shells. Frequently, these items find their way into Missy's paintings.

"I enjoy painting at the cottage more than anywhere else. My studio overlooks the bay, and early in the day, the only sounds I hear are the water lapping at the shore and eiderdown ducks calling out to each other. The island may be only a short ferry ride from the city, but on mornings like these, I feel a million miles away."

To keep the wooden wainscoting, *left*, and exposed beams from overpowering the living room, Missy chose upholstery fabric in bold, bright tones. *The Harbor at Vinalhaven*, *above*, by Missy Asen. **Missy's eye for color**, *right*, extends from her paintings done in acrylic paints and watercolors to her home as well.

Found in a local discount shop, *facing*, this inexpensive shadowbox table was originally dark wood and had a green velvet lining. Missy painted it white and then added a blue color wash. She used a permanent magic marker for the lettering before filling it with a layer of sand and the rewards of beachcombing. A colorful dhurrie rug from Pier 1 echoes the colors in the room. **Painted seafoam green**, *right*, with a cushion to match, a wicker chaise is the perfect spot to sketch ideas or to daydream.

Seashells bring nature indoors and anchor a room firmly on the shore.

A **whimsical sign**, *above*, from Missy's brother's restaurant hangs above the pantry door. **A tile-topped cooking island**, *facing*, rubbed with oil-based Benjamin Moore paint in green and blue, separates the kitchen from the dining room. The open storage shelves are the kind seen in many of the island's authentic Victorian cottages.

Topped with a vintage chenille bedspread, *above*, a family heirloom four-poster with pineapple finials sets a nostalgic mood. A mix of fabric patterns and the casual rose-motif drapes crowned by a found piece of carved wood impart old-fashioned summer cottage charm. **Missy gave the bath**, *facing*, a touch of elegance with a 1930s vanity fitted with a shell pink countertop, Victorian porcelain cross-handle faucets, and checkerboard vinyl sheeting by Mannington Floors. She sanded down a fire-damaged mirror bought for a song, protected the surface with sanding sealer, and hand-painted it to reflect the room's soft colors and bold checks.

Tropical Paradise

Key West, the southernmost in a long *chain of islands* off the tip of Florida, is well known as a haven for writers and artists. Its most famous visitor, *Ernest Hemingway*, owned a cottage on the island for about ten years. Several of his favorite haunts are described in detail, if not named, in the pages of his *classic novels*. 🌴 One place Hemingway captured is a saloon named Blue Heaven, which in Hemingway's time hosted cockfighting, gambling, and Friday night *boxing matches* on its patio—fights sometimes refereed by Hemingway himself.

Although Blue Heaven is now a family-friendly restaurant serving Caribbean cuisine, some things remain the same. Just as they did seventy years earlier, guests dining on the patio need to keep one eye out for falling coconuts and Spanish limes—and save the other eye for the island's famed wild chickens.

The free-roaming fowl, a quirky detail of life in Key West, are native to this historic town. Unlike the chickens, however, the island's "snowbirds" are a migratory species. Snowbirds, the nickname given to residents who winter on the island to escape cold weather to the north, are an integral part of the island's culture.

Jane and Tom Vetter have been snowbirds for many years, first as renters, then as homeowners. Tired of bone-chilling Missouri winters, the couple was attracted by Key West's tropical climate and its bohemian inhabitants. Next to them, other parts of Florida seemed "boring."

Half hidden behind traveler palms and a bougainvillea-covered fence, the Vetters' late-nineteenth-century cottage is built in Classical Revival style, featuring wide double porches and fluted columns. The two-story home was originally constructed for a sea captain from the Bahamas and had remained in his family for three generations.

"Since the cottage was designated as a historic site, we needed to get the approval of the Historic Architectural Review Commission before changing so much as a shutter," Jane recalls. "We were allowed to add an outdoor extension for dining in the back and a narrow pool along the side of the house because both locations were hidden from the street."

"I wanted our Key West haven to be a complete contrast to our Midwestern home," says Jane. "Our Missouri house is filled with dark antiques and conservative colors. The Key West cottage has white furniture and tropical motifs for a fresh, less formal look."

The cottage's living room furnishings, *left*, are from Bauer International's Royal Palm collection. A classic palm tree and tropical fruit pattern decorates the cushions on the rattan cricket club wing chairs, footrest, and mahogany bench cushions. One of Jane's prized artworks, by Santa Fe painter Kevin Sloan, hangs on the wall. Created in what the artist calls "magic realist" style, the landscape draws upon diverse imagery, including palm trees, hibiscus flowers, mangoes, and Roman ruins. **Coral, crabs, and fish silhouettes**, *below*, form the filigree on this custom carved window cornice—an ode to the cottage's waterside setting.

"White brings a serenity to our cottage that lends itself to the tropics."

The sea, a constant presence for island dwellers, greatly influenced her choice of accessories. Shells and tropical motifs are a subtle theme in every room.

"The cottage is totally open to the island breezes—no window screens, heat, or air conditioning," boasts Jane. When it rains, old-fashioned jalousies (hinged shutters with angled slats) keep out the rain.

Above window openings throughout the house are handcrafted wooden cornices. Each room's carved cornice sports a different theme, such as shells, dolphins, crabs, or tropical fruit. All are painted shiny white to contrast with the soft pastel wall colors.

"A wonderful friend, Lole Patlan, who lives in Missouri, made these cornices for us," Jane says. "It was a labor of love that took him three years to finish."

In the kitchen, a hand-carved palm tree extends prominently from the top storage shelf to the room's wood paneled ceiling. "This is my favorite part of the house," Jane admits. "With the kitchen open to the sitting room, garden, and the patio dining area, I don't feel cut off from Tom or our guests when we entertain."

Throughout the house, Florida heart pine wood floors make cleanup a snap. The wood comes from one-hundred-year-old river-reclaimed logs that have been hand planed and pegged, just as Victorian craftspersons used to do.

To create a visual flow from the indoor sitting area to the outdoor dining patio, Jane repeated the wood's blonde finish on her patio's concrete floor, scored the floor to resemble stone tiles, and stained it gold. She painted the beadboard in the coffered outdoor canopy a buttery shade of Benjamin Moore yellow.

Upstairs, the cottage's bedrooms are painted in tropical whites and furnished with antique beds, dressers, tables, and chairs. "White brings a serenity to our cottage that lends itself to the tropics," Jane explains. "It also has a cooling effect on the house."

Now that Jane and Tom have finished expanding and decorating their cottage, they have time to enjoy Key West's famed sunsets, to bicycle around the island, and to dine at the many fine—and funky—nearby restaurants.

"There's something irresistible about the laid-back lifestyle, sun, and sand that calls out to folks who live in less easy-going places," Jane concludes. "We tell our guests about the old Key West saying: once you get island sand in your shoes, you're bound to return here. That's what happened to us!"

Jane and her business partner drove two hundred miles to rescue a metal bed, *above*, during the Missouri floods of 1993. She then separated the footboard to create a pair of headboards, which she painted white. The hand-colored orchid botanicals came from a London flea market. **The wooden furniture** in this guestroom, *above right*, is all spray-painted a high gloss lacquer white, including two hand-carved twin beds Tom inherited from his grandmother. The antique rocker was a wedding present from a close relative. **Citrus green walls**, *right*, form a soothing backdrop for the vintage-look porcelain clawfoot tub and pedestal sink Jane ordered from the Renovator's Supply catalog. The coral and shell encrusted mirror, crafted by Jane herself, is a masterpiece. Cream, gold, and green Czechoslovakian lusterware from the 1940s in classical shapes is on display in a large hutch that doubles as a linen closet.

Harbor View Haven

The seaside cottages of Fairhaven, Massachusetts, are as welcome a sight today for beachgoers as they were for generations of sailors navigating treacherous fishing grounds along the *Cape Cod* coastline. This remarkable community along the shores of Buzzards Bay is a stone's throw from the *beach cottage* where Roberta Laprade grew up. "As a young girl," Roberta recalls, "I loved to visit a neighbor we called the 'shell shop lady.' She'd transformed her garage into a magical little store. As I browsed her stock of Florida shells and jewelry, *I dreamed of owning* my own cottage one day—maybe even hers."

Roberta grew up, got married, and raised three children in a landlocked New England suburb. But she still felt the pull of having the ocean as her backyard.

Roberta's mother still lived near town, and on her many visits, Roberta would sit in her favorite sandy spot and dream about living by the beach. One spring day, while driving along nearby Nasketucket Bay, she came upon a lovely place with a Sale Pending sign.

She called the real estate agent whose name was on the sign and told her that if the prospective buyer changed his mind, she'd be interested. Two months later the realtor called to say that the cottage was once again available; the buyer had backed out at the last moment.

Elated, Roberta called one of her daughters, and together they paid their first visit to what Roberta had already decided was her dream cottage. She wasn't prepared for the dreary, cobweb-filled rooms she found or for the almost complete lack of storage space, except for a tiny attic.

"On the other hand," she remembers, "the house did have a working fireplace and a pantry. And the windows were placed higher than normal so I'd have plenty of wall space to display my many collectibles. And the views of the marshes and bay were magnificent. That's what clinched the deal!"

Six months later, Roberta moved in. The cottage, built in 1953, had a closet-sized kitchen, an open dining and living area, a bedroom, and a narrow back room.

"Every surface in the house needed work," says Roberta, who sanded, primed, and painted every knotty pine board herself. For a light and airy look, she chose Martha Stewart paints—pale beige Sand Dune for the dining and living areas and aqua Morning Mist for the back room, which became her office.

A friend helped install hardwood floors and a sliding glass door in the bedroom. Once Roberta could see the actual beach from her bedroom, she started bringing a sense of the beach to the home's interior.

"I've finally found a fitting home for my collectibles," Roberta reflects with obvious contentment, waving her hand at a nostalgic display of shell-filled glass canning jars and bottles. "Many of these are treasures I bought myself from the 'shell lady' back when I was a child."

Besides the shells and jewelry she once saved her allowance to purchase, other childhood memories are found throughout the house. Family heirlooms, such as her mom's china cabinet and round oak table, and vintage linens are part of the cottage's eclectic mix—as are shabby-chic style furniture from the home décor shop she owns.

Most of the cottage's simple and stylish curtains are made from her collection of flea market textiles fastened to curtain rods with decorative clips. For privacy in her bedroom, Roberta sewed a tunnel pocket to an embossed French sheet and slipped it over an inexpensive rod. "I never cut old linens," she confides. "Instead, I fold them over or under to fit the height of a window."

Lined along the shelf of one of her dining room walls, however, is Roberta's favorite collectible: a pantry set from Czechoslovakia. Originally designed to hold kitchen staples, such as flour, sugar, oil, and vinegar (each canister bears the name of a different item), the beautifully decorated antique containers are regularly admired by visitors.

"I got these from one of the regular customers at my shop," she explains. "She found half of them at a nearby antiques auction. I fell in love with what she had, bought them, and decided they were too good to sell.

"A few days later she came in with the remaining pieces of the set. She saw them at a different auction—in a different town—and got them for me. Some things are just meant to be," Roberta concludes, "just like the way I found my own perfect little beach cottage!"

Most of the decorations and furniture, *above*, are from Roberta's shop, Enchanted Treasures, which she runs with her friend and partner, Martha LeComte. The oak china cabinet, however, is from her childhood home. It was originally used to store board games and galoshes. Now it safeguards precious china and antique linens. **To give the cottage the appearance** of more space and light, *facing above*, Roberta uses mirrors. Most have vintage frames that she has painted creamy white. **From the ceramic canister set**, *facing below*, to the hooked wool rug, roses set a romantic mood in the dining room. Even the claw-foot table and lovely press back chairs are draped in floral print fabric. Facetted crystal garlands cascade from the chandelier and candle stand for a hint of alluring sparkle.

One rainy winter weekend, *facing above*, Roberta turned bits and pieces of quaint fabric and trims into a trio of dreamy pillows. **In a nod to Hollywood's glory days**, *facing below*, beaded curtains mark the entranceway to the bedroom. Roberta's mother suggested painting the walls a fabulous coral color. The exact shade was borrowed from a pair of barkcloth drapes. **Eclectic treasures**, *above*, infuse Roberta's bedroom with a romantic sense of history. Vintage white and ecru linens and lacy bedding heighten the effect, as does a softly faded needlepoint tapestry featuring a floral garland. The animal print lampshade alludes to Roberta's wilder side.

A nostalgic postcard, *facing*, anchors this vine wreath decorated with gifts from the sea. **Roberta's favorite beach gems**, *above*, are displayed in a worthy shadowbox. When Roberta found it at a flea market, the frame was gold and the interior dark wood. What a difference a little paint can make! **Ocean blue bottles**, *right*, shells, sea glass, and strands of pearls are arranged to form a thrift shop mermaid's bounty.

The scene is set for an intimate tea party on the back deck. A rosy remnant purchased for pennies topped by a crisp vintage white cloth dresses up an inexpensive table. A trellis privacy screen gets a romantic makeover with fringed curtains and a shell garland.

With a seaside green-and-white color scheme, painted rockers, sisal rugs, and patchwork stitched by Susan, this enclosed porch offers the epitome in comfort. The sofas—big, sturdy, and great for hanging out in—are from Maine Cottage Furniture, a purveyor of home furnishings for casual, coastal, and second homes.

A Petite Retreat

No cars, no stores, no modern amusements—*summer vacation* on Little Diamond Island, Maine, is a welcome reminder of the way Americans used to enjoy themselves. ❧ Residents and visitors alike spend their *days at leisure:* gardening, reading, visiting neighbors, and swimming in the bay. The only time folks hurry on *Little Diamond* is when they walk across the sand bar that connects their island to Great Diamond Island, which, despite its name, is not much bigger than its neighbor.

Great Diamond's General Store offers fresh lobster rolls, homemade ice cream, and grocery items. Once the tide rises, the land bridge vanishes underneath the water of Casco Bay and you need to take the ferry back home.

Susan and Terry Palmer were renting a summer cottage on a nearby island when they decided they wanted a cottage they could call their own. They learned that an old Victorian summer house that was built in 1883 but hadn't been lived in for years was for sale on Little Diamond. Although the foundation needed shoring up, the house needed a new roof, and the whole place needed a paint job, Susan and Terry knew this was the cottage of their dreams.

"The cottage's walls were still original beadboard on the first floor and wide boards upstairs. Most of the woodwork had never been painted!" says Susan. "I knew right away this place had potential."

Not all of the home's reminders of bygone days were as pleasant, however. A previous owner had left behind a full-size glider plane, parked on the sun porch. Though the plane went out the door (actually, out the window openings) as soon as the Palmers bought the place, it took several years for the family to complete the renovations the house needed and to add a heating system for rainy spring and fall days.

"Terry and I both grew up spending summers at lakeside cottages. Every day was a great day," Susan remembers. "Now, when we go kayaking together, it's like we're kids again."

Susan felt that a simple, clean look was an integral part of a summer place. "A lot of what we've done was just to brighten the cottage up," she explains. "I am a big fan of Benjamin Moore's China White—it's clean and crisp and bright."

Before the Palmers moved in, the living room was very dark with varnished wood walls and ceilings, dark brown trim, and a floor painted a deep royal blue. "Even with all the window shades up in daytime, you could barely read a book!" Susan notes. "We painted the window trim and floors and left the magnificent varnished beadboard walls and ceilings intact." To turn up the wattage, she chose white furniture.

"Though I love vintage goods and antiques, I wanted comfortable, cozy, curl-up-in furniture and often antique furniture is not all that comfy." She chose couches and chairs slipcovered with natural color duckcloth for an easy, put-up-your-feet feel.

An advantage of decorating with white is that changing the décor is easy. "I like to change things around when the spirit moves me. That's part of the fun of decorating a cottage," she notes.

Several rooms were built around a favorite piece, like the Heywood-Wakefield round table on the sun porch. "The rattan legs and lashing make this cocktail table from the 1930s a cottage classic," Susan says. In the kitchen, an antique yellowware bowl collection and vintage labels are the focal points. Everyday dishes, pitchers, and cutlery are displayed on open shelving (a typical feature of Victorian cottage construction) and atop cabinets painted vibrant cottage blue. The display feels casual and unstudied, honest and unfussy—and the overall effect is beautiful.

Despite its mere 1,600 square feet of living space, the cottage boasts a living room with a wood-burning fireplace, an intimate dining room, a kitchen, a laundry room, three bedrooms, and a bath.

Until the weather turns cold in fall, however, the family's favorite place to gather is on the sun porch, which runs the entire length of the house. The porch's front and side are an expansive stretch of windows with breathtaking water views. "There's even room on the porch for a cozy office with a desk for two and bookcases," says Susan.

Upstairs, the whitewashed walls provide a classic backdrop for quilted coverlets and antique furniture. Fresh flowers from Susan's garden add spectacular seasonal color.

Like many summer residents, the Palmers find life so much fun on Little Diamond Island that they find it hard to leave. "It's a good thing that the water is turned off in October to keep the pipes from freezing. Otherwise we'd be tempted to stay here all year round!" Susan concludes.

What could be more casual, *facing*, than randomly painted chairs and shelves filled with yellowware bowls and sturdy ceramic dishes? Framed fruit crate and sardine tin labels from Susan's grandfather's Eastport, Maine, fishery tie the colors together handsomely.

A rainbow trio of towels, *above*, and a mussel shell wreath hang from humble pegs, providing a splash of coastal charm in the cottage's bathroom. Susan hot-glues shells together starting at the ring's outside edge. No base is needed.

A serene study in simplicity, *left*, the master bedroom exhibits a subtle red, white, and blue theme. Fashioned by artist and family friend Lynne Shulman, the fish sculpture above the bed is composed of driftwood, shells, and sea glass found on the local beaches around Casco Bay.

Daughter Abby's bedroom, *above*, offers respite to overnight guests, since she's now grown. The newly made quilts are worked in a traditional Bear Paw pattern. The vintage glass insulators and roadside sign came from Susan's favorite source for antiques—her parents' barn.

Lakeside Living

Celebrating Mardi Gras is a time-honored tradition for residents of the New Orleans. Vacationing on the cooler *northern shores* of Lake Pontchartrain is another customary annual event for many Crescent City natives. In 1990, Gwen Gasser and her husband Paul built their *summer cottage* on a waterfront parcel in the historic town of Mandeville. It reflects everything they love about *coastal living.* ◉ "Mandeville became a popular resort in the 1870s, when regular steamboat service was established to *ferry vacationers* across the 630-square mile lake," says Gwen. Hundreds of summer cottages cropped up along the *shore area,* known as Lewisburg.

Texture is the most sensory element—infusing

A hundred years of hurricanes have taken a toll on the oldest cottages, yet newer ones quickly replace those that are lost—and Seven Sisters, America's second oldest live oak tree, still stands proudly on a Mandeville side street. The tree provides a sense of continuity to area residents and is a living symbol of the tenacity with which Louisianans cling to their beloved state through thick and thin.

Like the Mandeville Live Oak, Gwen and Paul have deep roots in the state. They wanted their new cottage to become a seamless part of the town but they also wanted a house with contemporary design features.

"We hired Ricky Wendell, a well-respected Louisiana designer, to draft an informal cottage that reflected everything we loved about coastal living," remembers Gwen. "We wanted windows that could be thrown open to let in a breeze, a screened in porch, rooms with views of the water or garden, and a big outdoor space for entertaining."

Although the ten-room house Gwen and Paul Gasser built is larger than some older cottages nearby, the interior spaces feel no less warm and inviting. The 4,600 square feet of living space maintains an intimate scale, thanks to Paul's preference for angled ceilings and walls, small connecting rooms, and materials associated with boat building.

"We had the pine wall and floor planks specially milled in random widths to resemble those in older homes," Paul says. When a few were discovered to have cracks in them, the couple asked that the damaged boards be used instead of thrown away.

"Our contractor was amazed when we explained that we thought imperfections added character to a cottage," says Gwen impishly.

After eighteen months of construction, the house was finally ready for Gwen's finishing touches. Since the cou-

a room with offhand character and elegance.

ple wanted the lake to be the home's focal point, Gwen avoided decorating with bright colors.

"Most of the rooms are painted in a muted shade of green—a color I first saw on the wood walls of an old Mandeville bakery," explains Gwen. "I had our painter replicate the exact shade. Then I chose a complementary cream color for the floors and trim."

For the kitchen, which faces away from the water, Gwen selected a very pale misty blue color. The color reminded her of the waters of Lake Pontchartrain when the sky is overcast. Paneled with horizontal boards on the walls and perpendicular ones on the ceiling, the rectangular shaped kitchen was designed to be a gathering place for family and friends.

"My mother always welcomed guests into her kitchen to help cook, to watch her work, or just to taste the traditional Cajun fare she learned how to make from her mother," Gwen recalls. Like many who live just a stone's skip from water, the Gasser family menu often features the "catch of the day."

In 2005, sadly, Hurricane Katrina destroyed the couple's pier (which was their favorite fishing spot), their lovely garden, and a portion of the home's exterior. Gale force winds, however, were kinder to Lewisburg area residents than to those along other parts of Louisiana and the Gulf Coast.

Cleanup and rebuilding took many months, but today Mandeville's annual seafood festival is bigger and better than ever, and Spanish moss still clings to the Seven Sisters live oak. And although the Gassers have a healthy fear of future storms, they hope and believe that the town, the ancient oak tree, and their dream cottage will remain intact for future generations to admire and enjoy.

Carefully chosen tropical elements, *left*, and maritime motifs—some old, some new—capture the mood of a classic coastal cottage to a T. A sliding glass door with mullions leads to the quiet reading nook. French doors lead to a wide screened porch. The Gulf Coast–style dual ceiling fans are ideal in humid locations thanks to their vertically mounted motors.

The angled dining room ceiling, *below*, borrows freely from traditional lighthouse architecture. Barkcloth draperies in a Caribbean floral print add vertical interest and a hint of tropical color to the ten-foot-high windows. A stained glass panel depicting an old sailboat that hangs in one window has been in Paul Gasser's family for three generations.

Ships in bottles, *left*, from all over the world and examples of New England scrimshaw are just a few of the items Paul displays on the shelves surrounding the den's fireplace. On either side of the hearth, wide open doorways lead to the living room.

Examples of shell art, *above*, including boardwalk souvenir animal figures, intricate keepsake boxes, and amazing flower arrangements, grace a painted white buffet in the front hallway.

Gwen and Paul chose open shelves and cabinets, *facing*, with glass doors to give their kitchen a light and airy look. The pale blue plank walls and white cabinetry are punctuated with a colorful blend of imported ceramics and collectibles with a coastal theme. **The Gassers had a carpenter**, *right*, add wave-motif scrollwork brackets to the eating counter to give the kitchen island a more old-fashioned silhouette.

Furniture reminiscent of a West Indies home, *facing*, rattan, wicker, and bamboo—outfits the master bedroom. Gwen softens the look with vintage lace and chenille bed-spreads. **With the lake in view**, *above left*, soaking in the master bath-room's tub is very close to being outdoors. **Gwen created a masterpiece mirror**, *facing above*, by covering its original wood frame with natural aquarium gravel and then cluster-ing choice shells, sea glass, and coral into vignette "bouquets." She included a ceramic cherub as a

sentimental focal point. **A collection**, *right*, of shell-encrusted objects embellishes a shabby chic style vanity.

Vintage Inspiration

Finding a *classic beach cottage* for sale is uncommon. Discovering two authentic cottages is extraordinary. Located one behind the other, the pair of 1920s *Cape Cod style* cottages belonging to Janet and Don Walker are located in the prime resort area of Rehoboth Beach, Delaware. Each features tin roofs, cedar clapboard siding, and vintage window shutters—*prime examples* of what *early-twentieth-century* area *retreats* once looked like. Purchased back in 1976, one house was originally used by the couple as a weekend getaway, and the other served as guest quarters.

Summer is a state of mind that carries

When the Walkers moved to the shore full-time, Janet moved her antiques business in as well. The larger, front cottage became the couple's home. The smaller house was converted into Janet's office and shop, while the shady courtyard garden between the two homes turned into a combination alfresco dining room and a sales area for architectural salvage.

"Having an ever-changing assortment of vintage goods is exciting," Janet recounts. "Our grandchildren love that one week they might find old mosaic planters and a weathered rowboat, and another time, they can discover columns, windowless doorframes, and cement dogs."

The inside of the house, however, rarely changes. Even though Janet and Don live there year-round, the place still resembles a beach getaway. The color scheme is composed of sunny and sandy tones mixed with dune greens and watery blues.

The kitchen, remodeled in 2005, is the sole exception. Janet chose garnet red to contrast with the simple white cabinetry, appliances, and floor tiles. The room's new pressed tin ceiling, pendant fixtures and arched pass-through are in keeping with the cottage's humble style.

The Walkers firmly believe in maintaining the architectural integrity of their home and neighborhood. "True cottages are vanishing fast," notes Janet. "People are tearing them down and putting up bigger homes."

"Cottages have always evolved over time to meet their owners' needs, but we thought long and hard before adding a sunroom to the cottage," Don adds. While they could have built a bigger addition, they chose one that enclosed the existing porch and only slightly enlarged the cottage's footprint.

The new sunroom looks like it had always been part of the dwelling—a tribute to both the couple's restraint and

through the house in colors and textures.

their builder's skills. Flooded with light and designed for comfort, the new sixteen-by-sixteen-foot space is furnished with sturdy slipcovered seating in a "barely there" pale palette. The overall look radiates carefree summer pleasure.

Summertime is a state of mind that carries through the entire house. The living room calls to mind an old-time porch in which flaking paint on wood and wicker was a badge of honor. The bedroom takes its cue from a serene green bed frame that looks as if the cottage's original owners had left it there. The fact is, it could have been!

"As a child, I slept on that bed whenever I visited my grandmother; now my two grandsons, Benjamin and Jonah, sleep on it when they visit me. It's wonderful to be part of a continuing tradition," Janet reflects.

Despite loving everything about her snug cottage, Janet admits that having only 1,200 square feet of living space makes it hard to find room to display all of her cherished collections.

Having a cottage to spare, however, helps. Although officially the home of Janet's antique shop, called "Early Attic," the second cottage also offers room to showcase some of its owner's personal collections—and displaying those items, Janet has found, is good for business. It allows her customers to catch some of her enthusiasm for turning vintage goods into exciting vignettes—and encourages them to do likewise.

For someone like Janet who dearly loves historic cottages, getting others to see the beauty in the long forgotten objects they were once furnished with is an important first step in preserving the buildings themselves. By preserving, not destroying, these gems, generations to come will have the joy of discovering their own extraordinary homes—just as Janet and Don did more than thirty years ago.

Janet and Don chose windows in several shapes and sizes to take advantage of their sunroom's lofty dimensions. Having windows that face in three directions guarantees that the space is flooded with light from sunup to dusk. The neutral color palette creates a restful setting. A large model ship and a starfish border broach the subject of the nearby beach.

"I showcase vintage fabrics, especially barkcloth

In the cottage's cozy living room, *left*, vintage wicker chairs and a sofa are arranged around a table crafted from reclaimed wood. Floral pillows, a hand-hooked wool runner, and a patchwork quilt add to the nostalgic atmosphere. **Nothing says summer**, *below*, like a display of tin sand pails and watering cans. **White ironstone pitchers**, *right*, found a home in Janet's office. Displayed as tableaux, one per cubby, they take on monumental importance.

and floral quilts, for a nostalgic mood."

The successful mix of old and new, *facing*, in their kitchen makeover helped win the Walkers a coveted Rehoboth Beach Cottage and Town Award for Residential Renovation and Restoration. Removing the top of one wall made space for an eating counter supported by carved wooden corbels. **High-gloss red walls**, *above*, look dazzling against a sea of white and natural butcher-block countertops. The deep farmhouse sink lends a vintage touch.

Handed down from Janet's grandmother, *above*, the bed, bureau, mirror, and cane insert bench are ideal furnishings for the cottage. Both were brand-new in the 1920s. The chenille bedspread and pillows came from a local estate sale. **It's hard to miss the seaside theme**, *facing*, in the bathroom, with Janet's oldest and most valuable sand pails lining shelves, a lighthouse scene painted on the above-sink mirror, and a sailboat display shelf. You can almost hear the waves crashing against the shore, thanks to a clever mosaic tile floor border and stenciling just below the ceiling.

Guests are always welcome around the antique pine table. A set of flea market chairs boasts flirty seat cushions with short white skirts. Larger slipcovered parson's chairs anchor the table ends for the host and hostess. Carole's all-white dishes are easily mixed and matched.

The White House

For years, Carole and Bob Lindes anxiously awaited Friday afternoons. Friday was Carole and Bob's *favorite day of the week* because it meant their workweek was over and they could head for their Delaware shore beach cottage. They *cherished Saturdays* spent watching the Atlantic surf roll in. Sundays weren't bad either—until it was time to leave. ❋ "One of the best things about retiring was we no longer had to 'go home' every Sunday night. When we sold our house and *moved into the cottage,* it was one of the *happiest days of my life,"* Carole admits.

Carole's love of white, *below*, even carries over to her choice of her favorite birds. Several of her favorite swan collectibles grace the family room and its porch, including one that was handcrafted by her brother-in-law. Family heirlooms in oak and pine provide contrast to the all-white palette. The ready-made tab top curtains tied back with luxurious ivory bullion tassels are from Ikea.

Beadboard-covered cathedral ceilings, *right*, add a shipshape look to the welcoming great room. A sectional sofa and chairs covered in off-white linen sit in the center of the room. The sofa's placement offers an open invitation to Carole's grandchildren to roll over the back and squeeze in when a favorite show is on TV. Beautiful white ironstone platters add luster to the walls.

Built by a local contractor in 1995, the Lindes' waterside house sits atop pilings and has an "upside down" floor plan: the main living area and kitchen are on the top floor and most of the bedrooms are on the first floor. Outdoor decks and screened porches nearly double the plan's square footage, providing ample space for frequent entertaining, which the couple love to do.

Nicknamed "The White House" by family and friends, the cottage is decorated inside and out in a serene palette of ivory and cream.

"Deciding how to decorate the house was easy," Carole observes. "I have always loved the relaxing feel of white. It calms me. There's no competition with the colors of nature when you decorate with an all-white theme."

Duron's Shell White, a soft color that reflects the shimmering light off the ocean, was used on all of the walls throughout the house. Furniture is slipcovered in a variety of warm whites, and most of the accessories share Carole's favorite color choice.

"Even with seven grandchildren I have never strayed from my love of white. After our annual family reunion each Fourth of July, I just sweep the sand from the wood floors and toss the cotton duck and linen slipcovers in the wash," Carole boasts. "Talk about easy upkeep!"

The sturdy old pine tables and chests that add a sense of history to the fourteen-year-old cottage are impervious to wear, Carole asserts. "An extra scratch or mark on them just adds to their character!"

Some of Carole's fondest memories as a child are of visiting her grandparents' farm in the mountains of western Maryland. The rambling farmhouse had eight bedrooms, all usually filled with visiting cousins, aunts, and uncles. Her

uncle made a rustic wooden sign that hung on the large front porch, proclaiming this special place as "The Always Room Inn."

Today, this precious reminder of fun family times together hangs over the front entrance to Carole and Bob's cottage, welcoming another generation of family and friends.

The kitchen's cabinets were custom built by a carpenter who perfectly replicated an antique step-back cupboard from Carole and Bob's former home. "The divided glass doors were taken from an old home being razed. The bubble and waves of the antique glass make the room feel older than its actual age," Carole notes.

Like the sign, many of the cottage's wood furnishings come from her grandparents' farm. The rolltop desk in the first-floor family room once belonged to her great-

An antique headboard, *facing,* painted in Wal-Mart's soft white latex flat paint and waxed with Briwax backs a small daybed in the sitting room. Carole gently sanded the headboard to highlight its wood carvings. Old family photos in antique picture frames adorn the walls and provide a strong connection to the past.

A large beadboard island, *above,* topped with butcher block anchors the kitchen area. A metal pot rack found in a junk shop and sprayed white hangs from the ceiling. It holds vintage copper and cooking gear, as well as plants, dried herbs, and braided garlic ristras. Antique white porcelain glove forms provide a sense of whimsy.

grandmother. A nearby pine chest once held blankets but was rediscovered in the chicken house under layers of manure. The refinisher who meticulously scrubbed it all off told Carole that the neglect the chest had suffered was actually a good thing—because manure is a great wood preservative!

Several antiques Carole and Bob purchased also needed work before they could reach their full potential. A painted corner cupboard was stripped to reveal the original patina of the old pine. Now, it's the perfect anchor for the great room and a handy place to hide a television.

Another gem is a four-drawer chest Carole found without a top at an auction. She topped it with a white Carrara marble slab and back plate. The pearly grays running through the stone perfectly complement the painted hull of one of the model ships she collects.

While their coastal cottage is a long way geographically from the mountain farm that inspired much of the home's

decoration, the spirit of fun and family that Carole's grandparents encouraged is the same. Carole and Bob have only one rule they expect their guests to follow: don't hang wet towels and bathing suits on the front deck railings! Other than that, pretty much anything goes.

"I'm happiest during the two weeks over the Fourth of July when our children and grandchildren are all here. Then the house is full of activity and my favorite people," confides Carole.

Even if the weather is less than perfect, the top floor's open space magically stretches to accommodate everyone. The kitchen's large butcher-block island is always a gathering place.

Carole's collection of antique boxes is spread out throughout the house. They provide additional height for lamps, hold favorite photos, hide remote controls, and add interest to furniture in need of a lift.

Other unusual collectibles also provide relatives and guests with fascinating items to examine and converse about. Says Carole: "I love to search auctions and flea markets for the perfect piece of ironstone or old English pewter. Bob built a twenty-foot shelf above the windows of the great room for me so there's always room for one more item!"

Carole's love of cottage style led to a second career: a business called the Shop of the Four Sisters. Four times a year, Carole and her siblings completely decorate a coastal farmhouse and then sell everything in it.

"The sales have become so popular," she tells us, "the local fire marshal insists we hand out numbers to control the crowds in the house! Recently, we've added a large tent to hold more of our cottage chic finds." It's ironic to Carole that moving full-time to her retirement dream home has led, instead, to a blossoming second career!

Each of the four guest rooms, *facing*, is layered in vintage chenille throws, antique lace, and quilts. Varying shades of timeworn white combined with rich textures create a warm, cozy look. Here, a soft cream and beige toile fabric covers an old wicker headboard once headed for the refuse pile. The same fabric borders simple linen drapes from Ikea. A treasure trove of lace displayed in antique frames adorns the walls.

Old lace and chenille throws, *above*, dress the bed in the master bedroom. Antique alabaster lamps are softened with gathered shades that remind Carole of little girls in tutus going to a dance recital. The curtains are double layers of white voile sewn together, providing privacy but allowing for light to stream into the room. Pairs of tiebacks are sewn together, knotted on the ends, and tied to each wood curtain ring to create a dainty faux valance.

White tulle curtain panels, cinched in the middle with raffia, define the space on the screened porch. Carole glued seashells onto the raffia for a perfect seaside detail. Taupe Sunbrella fabric cushions corded in white give new life to the vintage rattan furniture (painted white, of course!).

Making Waves

Situated on the Delaware coast, this one-of-a-kind cottage is known to owners
Brooke and Rafael Steuart as *El Regalo* (Spanish for 'the gift').

"We never take owning a beach cottage for granted," says Brooke. "Rafael is
Cuban-American and *El Regalo* is the name he's always called the
cottage from the start." 🌴 Upon entering, a stairway *sporting bare
wood treads and risers* inlaid with tiny shimmering blue
and green tiles leads to the lower level. Bedrooms on this level offer an
intriguing *mix of personal* and playful furnishings reflecting
the family's *eclectic tastes*—and Brooke's talent for interior design.

Mixing round, square, curved, and straight

"When I graduated high school I spent two weeks sailing around the American Virgin Islands. The hot Caribbean sunshine made an incredible impression on me," recalls Brooke. On returning home, she painted her room in teal blues, mango greens, and fiery oranges—vibrant colors not often found in American homes at that time (even in teenagers' rooms).

Now that Brooke is an interior designer, she still favors tropical colors and watery hues in the rooms she creates. Her own beach cottage—in which a palpable passion for life at the shore fills the air—is no exception.

To truly appreciate the enviable ocean views their home offers, the Steuarts placed the main living area, in-

cluding the kitchen and great room, on its upper level. An open deck lets the family enjoy the best sightlines before bedtime.

"We love the way the areas flow into each other. It's ideal when we are entertaining, which is just about every weekend," Brooke notes. "A typical day starts with everyone having coffee and reading the newspaper on the deck or in the living room."

Later, after sunbathing on the beach or biking, friends and family casually drift from cocktails on the deck to dinner indoors to the fire pit outside, listening to music and watching the sun go down.

Although she wanted the cottage to feel small and cozy,

shapes makes a space feel vibrant.

Brooke chose a spacious gourmet kitchen because she felt their four children and their friends—and grown-ups as well—needed a place to hang out without getting in anyone else's way.

The kitchen's focal point is an island crafted of sunbleached cottage blue wood topped with an extraordinary granite surface. While the counter is made of stone, it doesn't appear heavy and solid. "I sometimes stare at the granite and get lost in its deep ocean blues, cool sky tones, and sparks of coral. It makes me feel completely refreshed, no matter how tired I may have been moments earlier," says Brooke.

The rectangular glass wall tiles that form the back-splash above the range and sink are also translucent. Like the ocean's waves, the tiles never look the same twice. A hypnotic green glass ledge forms a breakfast bar that separates the cooking quarter and the dining area. It's yet another reflective element that mimics the sea.

Tropical textures come into play in the dining area, where casual woven straw chairs line the sides of a table handpainted with Caribbean shell motifs. The end chairs have a more formal silhouette but are upholstered in a black-and-white jungle print. "There's nothing wrong with adding a little zebra print to any room!" Brooke advises.

A trio of ornate glass chandeliers and shell-filled jars displayed in a high niche draw the eye upward to appreci-

ate the soaring ceiling lines. Lit at night, the niche provides a warm glow. To conjure up the quirky architecture found in older cottages, Brooke added other recessed niches and angled walls throughout the house.

Another interesting feature of the cottage is the wide variety of places to sit and chat. Besides umbrella-shaded lounge chairs on the deck and sociable sofas in several rooms, there are even inviting spots between rooms. The house is so cleverly designed that a love seat and coffee table in a hallway do not intrude into the space at all.

In a cozy sitting room just off the kitchen, a sofa pops open into an extra bed for guests or baby-sitters. Drawing a pair of floor-to-ceiling draperies makes the room private. Tucked into a corner, a spiral staircase leads to the loft Rafael calls "kiddyland." Here, the couple's four children, Ruby (age 7), Talmadge (6), Reagan (4), and Rivers (3) sleep in end-to-end beds—summer camp style. Unlike most camps, however, "kiddyland" boasts a comfy section-al sofa and large-screen TV.

On the home's lower level, each of the adult bedrooms is decorated with a subtle theme: one features a vintage cottage look; another a South Sea feel; a third shouts "wel-come to the Eastern shore."

Like many traditional cottages, much of the home's furnishings are hand-me-downs. A charming handpainted bed, vanity, and dresser set in one of the guestrooms was Brooke's childhood bedroom furniture. "The set got its distressed look honestly through years of playful tumbling, teenage antics, and curling irons," Brooke admits. Several of the engravings and artworks in the cottage came from Brooke's father's farm. "The homeless treasures were in the barn when I rescued them," she notes. "They all need-ed reframing to bring out their special beauty."

The happy colors and touchable textures of Brooke and Rafael's home reflect perfectly the joyful lifestyle the family and their guests share. There's no thought of the precariousness a home perched on sand and pilings might suggest—just comfortable living, wonderful views, and a whole lot of love.

Contrasting dark and light, *left*, white-cushioned woven rattan chairs circle a dark wood table. The table is on wheels so that the room can be rearranged as entertaining and family life requires. **Crafted in Brazil of recycled wood**, *below*, found in the ruins of colonial era farmhouses, the dining table features a handpainted mural. It's a skillful work of art from the Roberta Shilling Collection. To offset the casual nature of the eclectic chairs, Brooke hung three glamorous crystal chandeliers above the table. They provide a fun contrast and generate gorgeous rainbows on the walls and floors.

Brooke chose rectangular glass tiles, *left*, for the kitchen's backsplash that reflect light in the same way that moving water does. An aqua molded-glass ledge, *above*, with a texturized wave pattern tops the peninsular. This functions as a raised breakfast counter on one side and a work surface on the other. Cloud white walls, facing, and a distressed Caribbean blue island make the cottage's family-sized kitchen feel friendly and intimate.

Flowers bloom in the guest-room, *left*, Brooke calls "Fun in the Sun." Here, an Asian-inspired black walnut bed from Pier 1 keeps company with a bold bedspread from Target, pillows from Pine Cone Hill's Sassy collection, and a rattan-framed mirror from a consignment shop.

Tongue-and-groove paneled walls and ship lantern lighting create a nautical mood in the breezy center hallway. The original heart pine flooring, here and throughout the cottage, was stripped and refinished to reveal its inner beauty.

Back River Beauty

Take an *early morning stroll* in Savannah, Georgia, and you'll notice that many residents wear dress shoes and shirts to take in their daily newspaper or walk their dogs. But travel eighteen miles to the east to Tybee Island, where many of these same folks own *beach cottages,* and you might conclude that not only do people in this part of Georgia not own dress shoes, but that they don't own any shoes at all! *Going barefoot* on Tybee Island means more than shedding your shoes. It's a symbol of a *slowed-down lifestyle* and an ability to appreciate life by the water, even if just for the weekend.

For fresh and spontaneous rooms,

Tybee, a barrier island, is dotted with historic cottages and colorful bungalows, many handed down from generation to generation. Some of the older homes, like the one Marcia and Ronnie Thompson own, were originally located elsewhere on the island and moved when hurricanes destroyed the shoreline.

"Our cottage was moved across from Tybee's ocean coastline to its present site on the Back River in the 1930s," recalls Marcia. "It had been abandoned for nearly twenty years when a real estate agent showed it to us in 1992. The house was a total wreck, with mold-stained walls and floors and roosting families of pigeons everywhere."

The Thompsons bought the place, intending to tear it down and build fresh. However, while interviewing builders, the couple had several chance encounters with longtime island residents. Each had an interesting story to tell about the place.

"It never occurred to me that it could be made livable," says Marcia. "But after learning about the home's rich history, I decided the cottage should be saved if it was at all possible."

Built in the nineteenth century, shortly after the railroad linked Tybee Island to the Georgia mainland, the cottage had once been the summer residence of a prominent Savannah family. Its wide front and back porches and central hallway are typical of low-country architecture in the coastal areas of the Carolinas and Georgia.

"It would have been less expensive to build a new home, but Marcia was determined to restore the place," notes Ronnie. "She did an amazing job."

Marcia's goal was to retain or restore the home's best features and to improve on those needing to be modernized. With the approval of architect Daniel E. Snyder, who has won numerous awards for his firm's historic preservation work on other Tybee Island cottages, two

display nature's beauty in all its forms.

interior walls were removed. The resulting great room includes a kitchen, an eating area, and a living room with French doors opening onto the screened-in verandah.

Now, just as it was more than a century ago, the home's main thoroughfare is a wood-paneled hallway. Doors at opposite ends channel welcoming breezes. The rear door opens onto a back porch with a view of a private dock and gazebo.

"When our children were younger, the gazebo was their favorite spot to picnic with their friends after a day of fishing from the dock," says Marcia. The home's many outdoor living spaces were one of the things that attracted Marcia to the cottage.

"One of the reasons I wanted a second home was to have a casual place for our children, my parents, and my grandmother to get together and enjoy each other's company," she continues. Her grandmother Sema Wilkes, who passed away in 2002, was known to generations of Savannah residents as the proprietor of one of the city's most beloved restaurants. The restaurant, called simply "Mrs. Wilkes' Dining Room," is still family-run and offers guests the finest in old-time Southern dining.

Through the years, Mrs. Wilkes gave Marcia and Ronnie many of her handcrafted chests, tables, and hutches. "My grandmother originally bought them to furnish a Savannah boardinghouse she ran before she opened her restaurant," Marcia notes.

These beautiful antiques are a sentimental reminder of her family's history and the era when the cottage was originally built. They demonstrate anew that the barefoot denizens of Tybee Island and the well-shod residents of Savannah have more in common than casual observers might imagine—a love of beauty, of preserving the past, and of the kind of careful craftsmanship found in many city homes, and in the Thompsons' Tybee Island sanctuary as well.

Spanning one entire side of the cottage, *left*, the verandah is furnished in newly re-painted white wicker. A table and chairs stands ready for afternoon tea—iced, of course! **The front porch of Beach Music Cottage**, *below*, greets the morning sun. Marcia borrowed the name from author Pat Conroy's best-selling novel.

A soothing yellow, white, and blue color scheme, *facing*, ties together the living room and kitchen area. The fireplace boasts Delft tiles and an impressive display of Marcia's blue and white porcelain collection. **Marcia framed a sheet music booklet**, *right*, as an ode to her island home. The booklet dates to the 1930s, when the cottage

was relocated to its current spot. The wooden legs of the butler's table are carved to resemble bamboo. **Thanks to an abundance of light-reflecting** white surfaces, *below left*, the kitchen looks as cheerful and fresh as the rest of the house. The wall cabinets' glass doors are as effective as having extra windows in making a room light and bright.

A small interior window, *above*, lets light into a corner of the kitchen. Vintage blue-and-white pottery, a brass ship's compass, a large nautilus shell, a hefty starfish, and tropical coral create a vignette with seafaring style.

The master bedroom, *left*, is kept cool with a splash of ocean blue. A remnant of shell-print upholstery fabric and a beach-theme oil painting provide additional seafaring accents.

This guest room's tropical color scheme, *above*, echoes the spectacular sunsets visible from the windows behind the bed. Well-loved family hand-me-downs make up the room's casually eclectic decor.

Beach Bound

Capturing a sense of place in your cottage's decor is like writing a love letter. The goal can either be a *celebration* of where you reside or a clever way to fantasize about your *dream destination.* ✳ On Casey Key, a barrier island off the coast of Sarasota, Florida, Nikki LaBelle's cottage is a *romantic ode to the sea and sand* just outside the doors. The color scheme, a combination of cool blues and whites, reflects the water.

The home's playful sense of style—a surfboard hangs above a flat-screen TV in the family room—captures Nikki's love of laid-back days spent on the beach.

"I'm always adding something new to the house."

Nikki admits that it wasn't love at first sight when she and her husband, Jeff, first set eyes on the house in 2002. They were driving around the island when they spotted a For Sale sign on a drab '80s house.

"The house wasn't too exciting, but the location was breathtaking," says Nikki. "Jeff loves to fish, boat, and surf—so the fact that the Gulf of Mexico was visible from the front door and Sarasota Bay from the back was a plus."

The LaBelles bought the property, knowing it would need to be renovated inside and out to create the sort of Old Florida cottage that Nikki wanted. As in the story "Sleeping Beauty," it took some time for Prince Charming—or in this case House Charming—to appear. The couple hired Bill DeRamo, a builder of custom luxury homes, to oversee the magical transformation.

In the first phase of remodeling, the cottage's exterior was overhauled, walls were removed, floor-to-ceiling

windows were added, surfaces were changed, and a new, old-fashioned kitchen were constructed. The upper floor was enlarged and improved during the second phase, which took an additional eight months to complete.

The once-austere front of the house now feels welcoming, with a pergola that leads to double doors and a wood-slat porch enclosed by a white picket fence. Painted a soft green, the house seems like a natural extension of the lush tropical garden.

"Bill replaced the existing wallboard with wood paneling. All of the ceilings and most of the walls are now tongue and groove strips painted white. The remaining walls are half beadboard," notes Jeff.

In the living room, Bill added beams to the vaulted ceiling to make the soaring space feel more intimate and created a fireplace with a wooden mantel and marble surround. Throughout the house, he installed doors, sinks, hardware, and pine floors that look like

As long as it's blue, I know it will fit."

they have been around a long time.

"The wood floors are awesome!" Nikki adds. "The dark-stained planks range from twelve to twenty inches. We even had our kids ride around on their bikes, skateboards, and scooters and walk around with sandy feet to make the wood look old and worn out in places."

Nikki decorated the cottage with a combination of flea market antiques and modern distressed pieces to complete the home's fairytale transformation. Whether it's a great photo, a piece of furniture, or a shell that she's found on the beach, if it calls out to Nikki, she'll find a place to use it—especially if it's blue. "I love the color blue, particularly the soft light shades. I even named one of our dogs Blue!" she says.

"I prefer to shop in stores that offer one-of-a-kind finds," she continues. "For vintage furniture with chipped paint, chandeliers, and other treasures, The Cat's Meow

in Venice, Florida, is one of my favorite places to shop."

Nikki admits she is always adding something new or rearranging what is already in the house. "That's the fun part of decorating. I adore everything in the cottage, but the handmade painted shell frames are really special. My sister Kim McLeod crafts them to sell. They are one of a kind and I love to use them for interesting pictures of my kids."

With four children, Regan (age 8), Noah (6), Xander (a year and a half), Bode (12 weeks old), and two dogs, including Blue, there are irresistible photographs to spare. The family also includes a camera-shy goldfish.

Today, Nikki and Jeff adore the house they've transformed. The cottage celebrates the seaside location they loved originally, the family they've created, Jeff's talent as an amateur gardener, and Nikki's skill as a decorator. Their home is a true love letter to themselves, to each other, and to those fortunate enough to be their guests!

Unlike modern furniture, *top*, which is frequently sold as sets, Nikki's dining suite is assembled from a variety of sources for added character. Reupholstered antique chairs accompany a custom-made table

that has been gently distressed. A stunning nineteenth-century French chandelier is reflected in a shell mirror crafted locally. **Nikki sets an artful table**, *facing below*, featuring Waterford crystal and vintage

blue-and-white transferware plates. **Light streams into the living room**, *above*, through floor-to-ceiling doors and windows. Decorated mainly in white with ocean blue accents, the space opens into the front garden on

one side and the dining room on the other. Nikki brings the beach indoors with a stunning hearth array of shells and coral. Many were collected on vacations in the Bahamas and Hawaii.

The childproof furnishings, *left*, in the family room include a distressed blue table, a white hutch, a French rocking chair, and a beadboard armoire, all purchased at The Cat's Meow in Venice, Florida. The sofas are slipcovered in white cotton for easy bleaching. Shell photo frames, a large surfboard, a nautical lantern, and a model ship link the cottage to its seaside location.

Nikki wraps the master bedroom, *facing*, in beachy stripes and faded florals in pale aqua and powder blue. Above the bed, a grand mirror from a gracious old beach hotel reflects a stunning sunset over the gulf. **Tucked behind a pair of French doors**, *below*, is Nikki's private retreat, an enameled iron soaking tub sheltered by a canopy of sheer gauze. The black-and-white marble floor tiles are arranged to produce a three-dimensional basketweave effect.

Coastal Reflections

The ocean is in Susan Wallace Barnes' blood. *Since childhood,* when her parents regularly drove the family from their landlocked northern California town to her grandparents' cottage on *Carmel Point,* Sue has felt most at home when by the water. Sue credits her grandfather for *cultivating her respect for nature* and for her desire to translate the mysteries of the sea *into works of art.* ✷ "We would walk down to the beach to the tidal pools," Sue recalls. "Whenever I would reach out to pick up something from the water, he'd tell me not to touch anything."

Imbuing everyday items with coastal flair

When they returned to grandfather's house, he'd hand her paper and pencil and tell her to draw what she had seen. "Once I started sketching, I never stopped," says Sue.

As an adult, Sue lived in Hawaii and Nantucket Island, and she paid extended visits to Mexico's Baja West and the Sea of Cortez and Nova Scotia's Cape Breton peninsula. Everywhere she went, she painted the world as she saw it.

Today, Sue's art appears on popular illustrated calendars, needlepoint designs, and notecards, offering millions of others the opportunity to share her skill in observation and experience the beauty of her world.

In 1994, Sue bought a cottage less than a mile from the one her grandfather once owned on Carmel Point. She was attracted as much by the unspoiled views from every window as by the quaint shingle-roofed house. The magnificent views were protected by the Big Sur Land trust,

Point Lobos Reserve, and Carmel River State Park, so she knew that she and her family would be able to enjoy them for many years to come.

The house is entered through a picturesque gate that opens to a walkway made of crushed shells leading to a Dutch door. The entranceway is so beautiful, it offers the sensation of a three-dimensional version of one of Sue's paintings.

"Keeping the top door open keeps the cottage cool and filled with light," Sue explains. "When I bought the house, everything was painted pink. I repainted the walls, beams, and ceilings in white. I had all the floors, except those in the bathroom, sanded down to natural wood. Those I painted an ocean blue."

On the kitchen blackboard, lyrics from a James Taylor song counsel that "the secret of life is enjoying the passage of time." Other quotes offer additional insights into the good life, including "learn something you didn't know

is the heart of laid-back cottage living.

yesterday; schedule time that's unaccounted for; and take your life and have it everywhere."

A tour of the five wood-paneled rooms makes it obvious that Sue has taken the last piece of advice to heart. Her home is a scrapbook of her life, passions, and travels.

Shells from Alaska, Bora Bora, and nearby Point Lobos are displayed in jars and containers, on open shelves, and in curio cabinets. Hats her Scottish ancestors wore, an African safari hat her father once donned, and several Sue herself has worn on her travels throughout the world hang on a wall.

Sue also displays unique rocks, paintings of the sea, hand-carved water birds, and books about her favorite subjects—the ocean and its largest denizens, whales. Even Sue's furnishings can be read like a travel diary.

The dining room table and leather-back chairs are from a church refectory in Mexico. "I bought that when

my sons were small and money was tight. The whole set cost only $125 in 1968," reminisces Sue.

The caned chairs in the kitchen were acquired almost thirty years later. They belonged to a talented Cape Cod needleworker who was close friends with Sue. Although the artist is no longer living, her daughter now works with Sue, turning many of her designs into needlepoint. Her company is called Cooper Oaks Design.

"When I lived in Nantucket, I met the most creative people on a daily basis. Everyone there paints, carves decoys, makes shell art, or weaves traditional baskets," Sue notes.

After living in many places, Sue is happy to call Carmel home. She loves the water and the abundant opportunities to observe wildlife in the coastal meadows and hills that surround the town.

"Every window of my house offers a different view. One bedroom is perfect for watching the sunrise, and

Filled with treasured paintings, lithographs and photos, sea glass, fossils, and other coastal gems, it's no wonder the living room is Sue's favorite place to relax and read. The teapot and cups are in Wedgwood's historic Flying Cloud pattern. A pair of whale sculptures suspended from the ceiling appear to be floating along in a leisurely manner.

the other is just right for watching the quail and other birds," Sue says. "We get bobcats, pumas, coyote, white tail deer, even an occasional wild boar. I hear cows on the hills above the cottage and sea lions on the beach below."

And her Carmel surroundings provide wonderful inspiration for her art. "These days, I'm sketching shore scenes, wading birds, boats, produce from the local farmer's market, garden vignettes, vintage cars, clotheslines, and lighthouses," says Sue.

Sue's dining room doubles as her drawing studio. Heirloom silver mint julep cups hold paint brushes, tubes of watercolors, drafting pens, inks, and Prisma colored pencils. The studio itself offers a display that's pretty enough to paint.

In addition to producing beautiful art, Sue uses her artistic talents to promote awareness of the ocean's fragile ecosystem and to sponsor youth programs in environmental studies.

She's been an active member of Whale Trust for more than six years and is currently collaborating with Jim Darling, Meagan Jones, and National Geographic photographer Flip Nicklin on a book about the ocean.

As fulfilling as Sue finds her own efforts to advance the appreciation of whales through Whale Trust and the Working Group for the Protection of Marine Mammals, an organization based in Switzerland, one of her proudest achievements took place much closer to home. One recent morning, Sue's daughter-in-law laughingly called from Portland, Oregon, to tell her about a question her son had asked. "Mom," he said, "Do you respect the water?"

Sue smiles, and then continues. "That's a very good thing for the earth's future."

This tabletop vignette, *facing above*, is an ode to the world's oceans. Sue created the "Kohola" illustration for Earth Island Institute International's *Whales Alive* conference, which was held in Maui. "Kohola" is the Hawaiian word for humpback whale. **A rustic country bench**, *facing below left*, is a delightful spot to read mail or converse with a friend. Each of the straw hats hung on the wall have a special significance for Sue, making a personal statement that is also practical. **A model ship tops a wall shelf**, *facing below right*, filled with a hand-gathered collection of shells. To make the best use of space, Sue glued several prime shells to the back of the display's surface. **A still life of rocks**, *above*, from French beaches, vintage glass floats collected by a friend in Kauai, and abalone shells found beachcombing in Carmel form a three-dimensional travel diary on a narrow table. The carving of a red-beaked Eastern Oyster Catcher was purchased in Maine.

Oriented toward sunrises framed perfectly through wide casement windows, *above*, the bed features a lively maritime pattern and cloud-white matelassé pillows. The reversible-weave coverlet was a gift from Sue's son and daughter-in-law, who found it in a small shop on France's Cape Ferrat peninsula. Photos of Sue's two sons share space with other memorabilia on a simple pine shelf. Assisted by her four grandchildren and her neighbor's daughter, Sue painted jellyfish, flip flops, octopus, and starfish on the wall-to-wall carpeting. **Glossy green fern fronds**, *facing above*, accent the bath's blue and white color palette. French linens from Jan De Luz's nearby shop maintain privacy and

await wet hands. **Sue based the painting**, *facing below*, on her "My Heart Will Always Be In A Cottage By The Sea" notecards on her own Carmel cottage and seaside gardens.

Resources

Artists

AUBRÉ DUNCAN
(302) 537-4171
www.aubre.com
Beach, boat, and landscape paintings

KEVIN SLOAN
(505) 982-0641
www.kevinsloan.com
Giclees, paintings, and prints

KIM MCLEOD
Loganandkai1@comcast.net
Custom shell frames

MISSY ASEN
(207) 781-4933
www.missyasen.com
Coastal acrylics and watercolors

SUE BARNES
Lifeguard Press
(800) 992-3006
www.lifeguardpress.com
Calendars and other stationery items

COOPER OAKS DESIGN
www.cooperoaksdesign.com
Handpainted needlepoint canvases

Design Services

BROOKE STEUART INTERIOR DESIGN
(301) 980-3920
www.brookesteuart.com

CANNARSA STRUCTURE AND DESIGN
(616) 610-0907
john@cannarsadesign.com

DANIEL E. SNYDER, ARCHITECT, P.C.
(912) 238-0410
www.snyderarchitect.com

GOODWIN HEART PINE COMPANY
(800) 336-3118
www.heartpine.com

MCCAULEY CONSTRUCTION
scottmccauley@yahoo.com

Furniture & Manufacturers

BAUER INTERNATIONAL
(843) 884-4007
www.bauerinternational.com
Furniture and tropical accessories

CLAIRE MURRAY
(866) 868-7001
www.clairemurray.com

FANIMATION
(866) 203-5392
www.fanimationlighting.com
Ceiling fans and lighting

HAVERTYS
www.havertys.com
Cottage-style wood furniture

HEYWOOD-WAKEFIELD
FURNITURE
(269) 756-9896
www.springdalefurnishings.com
Retro tables, chairs, and chests

MAINE COTTAGE FURNITURE
(888) 859-5522
www.mainecottage.com
Painted furniture

MODA FABRIC
(800) 527-9447
www.unitednotions.com
Reproduction vintage-look textiles

PINE CONE HILL
(800) 442-815
www.pineconehill.com
Bedding and home textiles

ROBERTA SHILLING
COLLECTION
(305) 477-7786
www.rscollection.com
Motif-painted furniture

ROBIN BRUCE/ROWE
FURNITURE, INC.
(540) 444-7693
www.robinbruce.com
Seating and accent pieces

Shops and Online Emporiums

BEACH DWELLING
(800) 941-9690
www.beachdwelling.com

ENCHANTED TREASURES
53 Main Street
Fairhaven, MA 02719
(508) 965-8224
www.enchantedtreasures.com

FINDINGS
San Carlos Street
Carmel, CA 93923
(831) 624-3700
Ribbons, fabric, and handmade accessories

JAN DE LUZ
4 East Carmel Valley Road
Carmel Valley, CA 93924
(831) 659-7966
www.jandeluz.com

SHOP OF THE FOUR SISTERS
517 Atlantic Avenue
Millville, DE 19967
(302) 541-8110
www.shopofthefoursisters.com

SUMMER COTTAGE ANTIQUES
153 Kentucky Street
Petaluma, CA 94952
(707) 776-2873
www.summercottageantiques.com

THE CAT'S MEOW
213 West Venice Avenue
Venice, FL 34285
(941) 445-5602
www.catsmeowinc.com

THE COTTAGE
219 West Market Street
Leesburg, VA 20175
(703) 443-0058
www.cottageatleesburg.com

THE OLD PAINTED COTTAGE
(805) 428-3903
www.theoldpaintedcottage.com
Vintage accessories

THE RUSTIC ROOSTER
930 South Coast Highway 101
Encinitas, CA 92024
(866) 787-8427
www.rusticrooster.com

Useful Products

BENJAMIN MOORE
www.benjaminmoore.com
Extensive palette of interior paint

BRIWAX
(800) 274-9299
www.briwaxwoodcare.com
Woodcare and refinishing products

KELLY-MOORE PAINTS
(888) 677-2468
www.kellymoore.com
Water-based and alkyd paints

PORTER PAINTS
(800) 332-6270
www.porterpaints.com
Designer and custom paint colors

RENOVATOR'S SUPPLY
(800) 659-2211
www.renovatorssupply.com
Antique and reproduction home goods

SEASHELL CITY
(888) 743-5524
www.seashellcity.com